The Way of the Heart

A STORY OF STRUGGLE, FAMILY, AND TRUE LOVE

ALDONA GRUPAS

Hasmark PUBLISHING INTERNATIONAL

Published by
Hasmark Publishing International
www.hasmarkpublishing.com
Copyright © 2021 Aldona Grupas
First Edition

Disclaimer

Permission should be addressed in writing to aldonagr@gmail.com

Editor: Brad Green
brad@hasmarkpublishing.com
Cover Artist & Layout Design: Anne Karklins
anne@hasmarkpublishing.com

ISBN 13: 978-1-989756-73-7
ISBN 10: 1989756735

TABLE OF CONTENTS

ACKNOWLEDGEMENTS

I could not have written this book without the help of my colleague, Asta Asker, and her husband, Firaz Asker. Asta and Firaz provided me with the story of love that became *The Way of the Heart*.

NOTE FROM THE AUTHOR

*I*n Denmark, Asta Asker completed Danish language courses while studying to become a senior health worker. She is my colleague and works in a residential home. She performs the duties of a health care worker.

BACKGROUND

The harsh period of modern history, beginning in the 1990s, changed the way of life for each of us.

Asta had everything; she was beautiful, charming, talented, and hard-working. But the thing she desired most in life was still missing – *true love*. No longer content to eke out a miserable existence, Asta gave up everything and put her trust in fate. After all, life is given only once!

After overcoming a series of obstacles, Asta achieved her desires. Now, she is ready to tell her story.

FOREWORD

Novels from the "dashing 90s" changed the lives of many women. During that time, our Asta—a young but already married woman who had become captured by worldly hardships—fought hard for her family every day. She honestly believed this is how things were supposed to be. However, at some point, young Asta realized that she could no longer wait for the changes that would bring new and better times to her life. The love in Asta's marriage was gone, and what remained was nothing more than trouble in the form of an irresponsible and selfish husband. Asta had developed an attitude of indifference. Their marriage carried on, primarily through the force of inertia. This could have gone on indefinitely if not for Mr. Chance who came along to intervene in her fate. Asta was offered a job in Denmark, which had completely turned her life upside down. It is during that time when Asta meets her love, who turns out to be an Arab man from Iraq. Real life is sometimes more amazing than any fairy tale. This is Asta's story.

1. THE STORY OF ASTA AND FIRAZ

Asta's Story

Copenhagen. A beautiful and happy northern city. It was morning, and sunshine winked through the window. I fed the family, walked the dog, and ran off to my nursing courses. Not so long ago I decided to acquire a new profession. Soon after was the defence of a diploma—probably the last diploma in my life. Although, as they say, *never say never.*

As I pondered the events that brought me to this place in life, I suddenly recalled the story of the Austrian writer, Edmund Josef von Horváth. A clairvoyant had predicted that Edmund's fate would be decided in Paris. It wasn't long before the writer found himself in the city on the Seine for business, and while there, he visited the Louvre and other famous Parisian sights. At some point, he decided to take a walk along the Champs Elysees, and what do you think happened? A thunderstorm suddenly broke out, and Edmund took refuge under a tree. As he sheltered from the storm, lightning struck the tree where he stood, and he was killed by a large falling branch!

Here is a decision of fate worth marvelling at.

Like Edmund, I also met with a clairvoyant who predicted a happy life abroad for me. I smiled to myself in disbelief. Surprisingly, her prediction came true! It was not just the clairvoyant's prediction that brought me here, but also the help of my girlfriend. I could have never imagined that this decision would change my life so much.

2. FAMILY

Asta's Story

I was born in Lithuania in 1972, in the small provincial town of Panevezys. There are many small towns like this one on the coast; clean and comfortable towns, where almost everyone knows each other.

Our city was different from others because of our factories. There was the Ekranas factory, where TVs were made. There was a sugar factory, as well as the Sema factory, which produced alcohol. And there was a glass factory which produced very beautiful products, including vases, candlesticks, and figurines.

I was one year and eight months old when my father died. Mom was left alone with three children, my two brothers and me. Of course, I don't remember my father. I only know him from the photographs and stories my mother shared with us. Because he left us so early, I did not feel my father's love and I cannot imagine what it could be like.

I grew up like all children, in the nursery, then in school. I was not an excellent student, but I had many friends. They defended me, even asking teachers to give me higher grades. Sometimes this actually worked.

In general, our class was friendly, and I could always count on the help of others. As a result, even at the age of sixteen and for a long time after, I played the part of a defenceless little girl in order to receive care and affection from guys.

My older brothers were also my protectors, and everyone was aware of that. I felt safe everywhere I went.

One evening I went to a disco with my friends. There was a tall, handsome man there that evening, and everyone was peeking at him. I was no exception!

After the disco, he said to me, "Asta, would you like to keep me company? Come on, take a walk around the city with me." Of course, I agreed. I was happy with his attention. He was an older guy, an athlete, and very popular among girls … and he chose me!

I was bursting with pride. It may not have been love at first sight, but a spark of mutual interest flared between us from the second our eyes first met.

After this first evening, we began dating regularly. I treasured our friendship. We went to the cinema, or to visit friends. But over time, I noticed a problem. He loved to drink and drink a lot, and when he did, he would become violent.

Despite the warning signs, I remained fascinated by him and did not pay attention to these problems. With me, he was gentle and affable.

We dated for two years and decided to get married. I had turned eighteen years old, and he was twenty-four. After living together for some time, I began to dislike his frequent nights out with friends, drinking and staying out until the morning.

But still, I didn't react seriously. At that time, I worked in a nursery as a nursery assistant; my work required a lot of my time and attention. He also worked but changed jobs often, and eventually lost his job completely.

When we got married, we decided that we would first live for ourselves and have children later. In the beginning, our neighbours gossiped. "Why don't they have children?" When we initially got married, it was rumoured that I was already pregnant. "That's why she got married!" The same gossiping grannies would chat about completely different things at different times. What can you do with such a mentality?

And so, we lived like this, under the gossip and constant evaluation. But I'm strong, and I'm used to making decisions for myself.

Finally, the moment came; my husband and I made the mutual decision to have a child. After living together for three years, we had a son in 1994. My husband was delighted! The pregnancy was challenging, and the birth was very difficult. I barely survived, but I was happy because we had a son. Rumours began to spread around the city again. They said the baby almost turned its head during childbirth.

My husband was overjoyed! Though the birth was very difficult, he did not leave my side for a second. He patiently wooed me, and worried about our son. It was very nice.

When my son began to grow older, I entered the conservatory. Despite the difficulties, I finished my studies.

But the good stages of life sometimes come to an end.

I lost my job some time later. My husband had begun to travel abroad to earn money, but more often than not he came home without it. There were always excuses for why he was not paid. We decided that if the customers don't pay, then he'd be better at home with his family. So, he stayed at home.

3. FAMILY

Firaz's Story

I was born into an Arab-Armenian family in the city of Baghdad, Iraq. My mother's parents came to Iraq during the Armenian-Turkish conflict. My father and mother met in Baghdad, and soon fell in love.

Besides myself, there was another son and two daughters in our family. I was the youngest.

My father and mother were both Christians, so there were never religious differences in the family. After all, the Middle East is the cradle of Christianity. It was here that the religion originated and then spread throughout the world.

In the period prior to the establishment of Abbasid rule in AD 750, pastoral Kurds moved into upper Mesopotamia from Persian Azerbaijan, taking advantage of an unstable situation. Cities in northern and northeastern ancient Assyria were raided and attacked by the Kurds.

The Christians of Iraq are considered to be one of the oldest Christian communities in the world. The vast majority of

Iraqi Christians are indigenous Eastern Aramaic-speaking ethnic Assyrians. Non-Syriac Iraqi Christians are largely Arab Christians and Armenians, and a very small minority of Kurdish and Iraqi Turkmen Christians.

Armenians usually say that each separate family is a state within a state, meaning each family has its own laws that are independent of the government and the president. The father is considered the leader of the family. His opinions, decisions, and desires are not deliberated. These rules are normal in the Arab world.

My family lived in abundance. We had a house in Baghdad, and our financial condition was very good.

Our family respected the culture and religion of their ancestors and adhered to all traditions.

4. TIME FOR WORRY

Asta's Story

I have not seen war, but I know what hunger is.

My husband and I, together with our child, lived with my mother on her small pension. It was terrible!

It was then that I came to the realization that money is a great universal evil. My husband and I had been living together for almost nine years, and by this time our son was six years old. These nine years had been full of scandals revolving around money. For the last three years, nearly all of our quarrels were about money.

At that time, my cousin lived in Denmark. She married a Danish man and left for a better life. In my family, a discord was brewing, and my patience was running out. I did not see a way out. We were forever in debt and had no work, and my mother's pension was not enough to sustain us. There was endless conflict at home, and our home was like hell. Sometimes in the morning I had nothing to feed our son. I'm grateful to the friends who helped. Some gave potatoes and some gave bread, or other helpful items.

5. TROUBLE IN IRAQ

Firaz's Story

At that time, the world was in a fever.

There was a coup in our country, followed by war. Terrorists began to persecute Christians, saying that they did not belong in the country because Iraq belongs to Muslims.

The goal of these terrorists was to expel all Christians from Iraq, and they persecuted us in every possible way. They used cars as bombs near temples, and they beat or even mutilated Christians. As a result, many people died. Activists of the terrorist group issued a statement in which they declared their organization as Islamic and affirmed that the attacks were punishment for the Crusades against Islam and Muslims.

Life became extremely difficult. Many Christians gradually began to leave Iraq, heading to places like Syria, Australia, or European countries. Some Iraqi Armenians emigrated to Armenia. My parents worried about the safety of our family.

My father decided to leave Iraq because it was becoming more and more dangerous to live there. My older sister and I were among the first to leave for Europe. We were young, had no families, and therefore no constraints. We decided that changing everything in our lives would be much easier.

6. A LONG WAY TO HAPPINESS

Asta's Story

I eventually became tired of all this struggle and called my cousin in Denmark, asking her to find me work. That was in 2001. She helped me find a job, and so I began to get ready to work abroad. Guess what happened then?

The family all agreed that I should go, but neighbours and other acquaintances began to condemn me, putting me on par with prostitutes.

Why do people have such a mentality? If a man goes to work, this is normal. Even if he doesn't earn any money, it's still commendable. But if a woman is going to go to work in order to save her family from poverty, then this is prostitution.

But I am a strong woman. Debt, hunger, and the responsibility of caring for my child tempered me. I accepted the opportunity to remove myself from the grip of my gossiping neighbours, and I left for Denmark.

My cousin helped me a lot when I arrived in Denmark. I did not know the language and I understood that no one would give me a well-paying job. I washed dishes, cleaned hotel rooms, and worked in fields.

At that time, my English was non-existent, despite the fact that I had been taught it in school. In the end, I did not learn much at all. I was very loved by my classmates, and they begged the teacher to give me a good grade, which he did. These marks were clearly overestimated. I am not proud of it, but it was so.

In 2001, I went to Denmark through Sweden. I spent sixteen long hours alone on the ferry. No one accompanied me. At that time, I did not suspect that I was sailing towards destiny.

7. MEETING DESTINY

Asta's Story

*T*he ferry from Lithuania went only to Sweden, so my cousin came to meet me from Denmark.

In those years, there was still no European Union, so countries did not allow tourists in as easily as they do now. Each person entering a country needed to show that they have enough money to live in the country. Usually, a considerable amount of money was required. To get around this law, a resident would need to vouch for you by writing a statement that they were ready to support you.

When I entered Sweden, customs officers immediately began asking me questions, but I did not understand the language and could not answer. They interrogated me for a long time but could not achieve anything intelligible. After some time, I finally realized that they were wondering if anyone was coming to meet me. I nodded and wrote my cousin's name. They immediately called her over the speakerphone. She came up and the customs officers checked the documents and let us go.

And so, I continued to Denmark, worked, earned money, and returned. I paid off our debts, and again we were left without a penny for a soul. All over again, we were sitting on zeros. After all, work in Denmark was seasonal. We were again overcome by poverty, from which we had no idea how to get out.

My love and my patience began to die sequentially. I began to increasingly break down at home. I scolded myself for this but continued out of despair.

One afternoon, I met a friend by chance. She was one of those people who, it seemed to us, lived where money grows right on the trees, and all you needed to do was make an effort to grab it.

She suggested that I go with her to try to change my luck. I was depressed and did not see a way out of my current circumstance. It was impossible to fix anything here in Lithuania in those years, so I decided to leave. I thought it would help to earn money, and the separation could possibly help to warm the relationship with my husband. In short, I decided to change everything.

Led by the hand of my cousin, I began my new life. She helped me find a job at a cleaning company. The work was difficult.

The owner of the company was an Arab man, but his wife was Russian so he could communicate a little in Russian. It was my salvation. I could speak and understand.

The Arab man and his wife were cheerful people and were constantly up to something. On the first day we met, they drove me in a car to show me Copenhagen. I spent almost four hours with them. My cousin became worried with my sudden disappearance and almost called the police. It's good that we managed to return on time!

This Arab man was a very good and respected person. Later, when I had been working for them, he helped me a lot. Being able to speak some Russian, he was able to explain everything intelligibly. Unfortunately, he could not stay at my side all the time during my work.

He introduced me to a guy from Africa who was supposed to help me understand my responsibilities, but he spoke only in English.

When the Arab man left (he was the boss), a language barrier arose between me and the African man. I did not understand a single word, and I stood like a pillar. He said something to me, and I just blinked my eyes. Apparently, the stress had blocked all my senses at once. It seemed to me that I did not know how to speak at all, even my own native language. As soon as I opened my mouth, a chicken cackling and an inarticulate moo burst from my chest. His eyes got bigger and bigger. I still couldn't speak.

I probably have a good guardian angel. When the African man saw that I was having difficulty, he took my hand, took me to a room, put a vacuum cleaner in his hands, and showed me how to handle it. It was like a stone fell from my soul, and I exhaled.

Nothing unusual was required of me. And under the quiet rumbling of a vacuum cleaner, I began to carry out my daily work.

The boss came and talked with the African man. Years later, I found out that he said, "Who did you bring me? She does not understand anything and does not know how to do anything!" The African man demanded that I be fired the very next day, but the boss reassured him and asked him to be patient.

When I tell this story now, it's funny for me. But at the time, I became confused. What is this tetanus? Where did this condition come from, and what to do with it?

After years of working together, recalling my labour problems, the African and I both laughed to tears.

I worked twelve to fourteen hours per day and earned a good salary, with which I could buy what I wanted. And then I had a revelation.

I remembered my husband. He also travelled abroad and received money for his work. But where did his money disappear to, and why did he bring home nothing? He drank it away!

I had only worked for two months and already earned a decent amount. Part of this money was spent on paying off debts. Then I bought a TV, and for the first time in my life, I allowed myself a bottle of good perfume. It was a French perfume, Miss Dior. It's a common thing for many women, but for me it brought unimaginable happiness! I was proud of myself and was filled with a beautiful, gentle female feeling.

Later I came back for seasonal work in a restaurant. I prepared the hall for the arrival of guests and served banquet tables. I worked five seasons she means five seasons, not in one part, she went home and cam back for oyher season. with no days off, in daily shifts of nine, ten, or even twelve hours straight. At first, I lived with my cousin, and then, having already begun to earn stable income, I rented a room of my own.

8. A DECISION TO CHANGE FATE

Asta's Story

*I*n Lithuania, at the private house where we lived with my mother, there was a small garden. Returning home after several months of work in Europe, I saw that the grass had grown waist-high, although my husband remained at home with no responsibilities. It was difficult to get any help from him. He much preferred to read or watch TV. Our child was raised by my mother.

Of course, my ex-husband has some good qualities. He was very attentive to me and the baby after giving birth, and he had helped my brother in a difficult situation. But the time came when this was not enough. Life with him had become unbearable. You can't continue to live with someone only based on their past achievements.

My love and patience for him was gone. I began to increasingly break down at home. I scolded myself for this, but I continued to work things out. Conflicts continued. He tried to stop drinking, but again broke down.

Conflicts had gradually become an integral part of our family life. They happened regularly, whether he was drunk or sober. It was terrible. He did not raise his hand to me, but dishes often flew around the house. Under the clinking of dishes, his aggression was on full display.

The conflict that finally put an end to our relationship happened because of a little thing. We yelled at each other, and our son came up and stood between us. He extended his arms and wept, pleading, "Be human! Stop!"

I am not one of those women who will clog into a corner and wait with tears in their eyes until everything settles down. I do not allow myself to be offended. This situation had become decisive for me. If I have already decided to start a new life, then I will do it. It was 2005.

9. 2005

Asta's Story

My friend and I went to buy tickets to Denmark, which were sold at ticket offices at the station. At the ticket office, I suddenly changed my mind, and turning to my friend, I said, "I will not go." My friend was taken aback. "Are you crazy? What happened?" she said.

The cashier looked at us both with displeasure and waited. I turned and left the ticket office and walked to the street. My friend was in disbelief and ran after me. She caught up to me and began to ask why I was doing this, and what had happened. I kept saying only one thing, "I don't want to go there. I'm tired. I have to work like a horse. I'm tired." My friend was persistent and persuaded me until I agreed. I said, "Ok, but this is my last trip."

I returned home in a bad mood. My soul was torn from the thought of breaking up my family. We sat on the sofa in the room, sullen. My husband sat across from me. I said to him, "Don't let me go to Denmark. I beg you." He replied, "How can I stop you? You have been working there for so many years. You are an adult; you must decide for yourself!"

When I recall these moments, I am grateful that neither my previous or current husband closed me in a cage and that they did not infringe on my freedom.

Of course, I also have my own priorities in relationships. I value my dignity, and I respect my husband. But I enjoy being free in my endeavours, activities, and ideas.

I was going back to work, but literally two weeks before departure, my friend asked me to accompany her to a fortune-teller.

When we arrived, she suggested, "Do you want to go to the fortune teller so that she will tell you your fortune?" I answered, "No, I'll wait for you at the door."

When the fortune-teller finished the session with my friend, she came out and saw me. She asked if I wanted her to tell my fortune. I refused, but she persistently offered her services, even saying that she would not take my money. "It's not about the money," I answered, but for some reason I agreed.

And so, she told me everything about my husband and about my life. I listened and thought to myself: *You all say that but look at the reaction of a person. You speak and speak, and I will sit and listen.*" My indifference almost put me to sleep.

Then suddenly she said, "You think you are only going abroad to work, but you will stay there forever. If you stay with your current husband, you will live as long as you want, and he will never leave you. But I see that a lot of love will come to your life. Very strong and mutual love, and you will have a daughter."

Of course, I laughed. What nonsense! I already have a family and I will never leave them!

I even joked when I told my friend that now I can't go! Great love awaits me there!

It turns out that my love *was* waiting for me there. Never say never.

But, nevertheless, the fortune-teller changed my mood. I began to act like a stupid little child. When we arrived in Copenhagen, I ran from column to column at the airport, shouting, "Where is my love? Which column is he hiding behind?"

My friend was ashamed of me. She tried to reassure me, saying that I should not shock people with such behaviour.

10. BACK IN DENMARK

Asta's Story

I returned to work and immediately enrolled in Danish courses. I wanted to communicate with the people who surrounded me! I wanted to understand what the people around were saying. I studied the language with passion and became more confident in myself. I could already understand when people asked me questions, and I could even answer some. At work, little by little, I began to communicate with the locals. I spent leisure time with friends.

It was very difficult mentally. One thing I was sure of was that my son was in good hands back home. He remained with my mother and husband.

Emotionally, I was thrown from side to side. I became depressed and began to miss them. It was especially difficult during the holidays, on Mother's Day or Christmas, for example. I was worried that my son was growing up without a mother. Periodically, I had panic attacks. It was very difficult. My mother reassured me. She is a great woman with a divine soul.

At that moment, I realized that no one who leaves their family and goes abroad to earn money does so with a good life at home.

11. SEARCHING FOR MY PLACE IN LIFE

Firaz's Story

*I*n 1997, my elder sister and I left Iraq.

First, we went to Jordan, where our uncle lived. We stayed in Jordan for six months, until we found a way to immigrate to Europe.

We got our first visa to Romania, where we spent about one month. But in this country, we encountered certain difficulties. At the time, Romania was socialist (under the influence of the USSR). It was quite difficult to settle there, and we were not there by our own choice.

We celebrated the new year of 1998 in Romania, and a few days later we left for work in Germany. However, we stayed there for only about one month.

It was a difficult time for emigration. Everyone had problems with passports, and we were stopped by police and checked every now and then. We decided once again to change our country.

12. SWEDEN AND DENMARK

Firaz's Story

Sweden is a beautiful and rich country, but unfortunately, they were strict with refugees. There were some criteria which we could not meet in order to stay there legally.

We had been visiting relatives for some time and thinking, *where to next?* I wanted to settle already, to have clearer prospects and a more stable life. We moved from Denmark to Sweden, but, alas, we were caught by the Swedish police and deported back to Denmark. The long movement through several countries was due to our lack of refugee status, and it took a lot of time to draw up documents. We needed to legalize our residency in Europe.

My sister and I arrived in Denmark in 1998, but it wasn't until much later that we received our refugee status. Denmark is also not a country that easily accepts refugees.

To obtain legal status, you must first live in a special refugee camp, learn the language, and only then can you look for work.

We spent six months in the camp before receiving a residency permit for Denmark. It was a difficult time.

13. REFUGEE CAMP

Firaz's Story

What is a refugee camp? This is a small area near the forest, filled with a large number of containers equipped with rooms. Immigrants live in these conditions. We lived in containers.

We did not have friends or relatives in Denmark. We began to look for work, but unfortunately, without knowing the language, were unable to find anything.

Over time, I began to look for my compatriots. When I found them, they advised me to go to the mosque to ask for help there.

Of course, looking at us, no one would doubt that we were Muslims. But I did not go to the mosque because I was afraid to admit that I am an Orthodox Christian.

At the camp, my sister and I became friends with some people who advised us to go to restaurants, house cleaning companies, and hotels, or to try to get a job as peddlers of newspapers or food.

My sister and I agreed on everything in order to find a job. I understood that we had to start somewhere. We had to learn the language. And we learned! We went to school where we studied Danish for two years. Danish was a difficult language for us, but we have overcome this barrier.

Without the language you are no one, and this is understandable. While studying, I found a job. I settled in a restaurant, washed dishes, cleaned, and delivered orders to homes.

14. NEW LIFE

Firaz's Story

I had to overcome many thresholds, the most important of which was overcoming myself. I grew up in a wealthy family. My mom never worked. I did not know how to wash dishes, clean rooms, or deliver food. We had a servant who did all this for us.

But occasionally, the time comes when you have to rethink your values and priorities. It was very difficult for me to overcome my conceit and change my outlook on life. I never imagined that my life would turn around so quickly. I felt immensely sorry for myself, and sometimes I cried.

But then I began to think that this is a new life, and that I had to start somewhere. I shut out my negative thoughts so that they would not interfere and started to work.

I worked and studied at the same time. Yes, it was difficult, but now I had a goal. I wanted to settle in this country.

15. JOB

Firaz's Story

When I graduated from Danish language training, I found a position at the post office. They gave me a bicycle, and I became a postman. Everything seemed to be simple. For the first time in Denmark, I was really happy. It was my first normal and well-paid job. All the postal workers were Danes. I was the only foreigner. I made new friends, and we are still friends to this day.

We received our official status giving us the right to legal residency in Denmark, and with the money I earned, my sister and I were able to leave the camp and rent an apart-ment. In this apartment we spent six years of our new life.

16. BAGHDAD

Firaz's Story

*M*eanwhile, my parents sold their house in Baghdad and, together with my second sister's family, moved to live in Jordan. There they rented a house while my father was alive, but he later died and is buried in Jordan.

After the death of my father, my sister's family, together with my mother, decided to recover in America. They left for California, where they live to this day.

I made friends with a Danish girl. She was only a friend. We didn't live together and didn't contemplate love, since I had never considered creating a family with a woman of a different nationality. This was strictly prohibited in our family. Families should be exclusively Arab and live according to Arabic customs. Therefore, a future together with a girl from Denmark was not even discussed. With that, we parted.

17. DEFINITIONS OF DESTINY

Asta's Story

A new country, new friends, and a new me. There were so many interesting things around, and I wanted to learn more about life in this new place. Before that point, I had only lived in Lithuania and visited Moscow. That was the extent of my travels.

While studying the language, I also became acquainted with the culture of the Danish people. My previous knowledge of this country was limited to geographical data and the tales of Hans Christian Andersen.

For example, I learned that Andersen was not only the author of fairy tales and poems, but also a virtuoso who worked miracles with scissors and paper. He carved outlines, patterns of extraordinary beauty, folded and interlaced paper garlands, and made entire bouquets of paper flowers. One of his creations, a woven paper heart, is very popular in Denmark. They fold it, cut it out, use it to decorate the home, hang it on Christmas trees or walls, or in windows as decoration.

In addition, my friends and I walked a lot, getting to know Copenhagen and its environment.

One of my friends had an Arab boyfriend, a very friendly guy. As it turned out, her boyfriend was friends with the person who would become my second husband. He is the person who introduced us.

One day, my friend invited me to visit her boyfriend, and she said that his friend would also be there. I agreed to come and have fun with friends. In the yard, in spring, hormones were at play, bringing nostalgia for my family back home.

I joined my friend and met the others. The man they introduced me to was not very tall, even shorter than me, and of Arab descent. His name was Firaz.

I didn't have any emotions.

I thought, *he's short, and he's an Arab, a Muslim.* My brothers and my first husband are tall and handsome men, real heroes.

But I did not come to this gathering in search of a husband. I only came to talk and enjoy myself.

That evening, the funeral of Pope John Paul II was on television. It was 2005.

I glanced at Firaz. He was watching the funeral on TV so carefully that I became curious, and I asked, "This is the burial of the Christian pope. You are a Muslim. What interest do you see in this?"

To our surprise, he replied that he was not a Muslim, but an Orthodox Christian. What a surprise! I have nothing against Muslims, but my prejudices, nourished by rumours of unhappy families, are somewhat beyond my control. Honestly, I began to look at Firaz differently in that moment.

A lively conversation immediately ensued. We were interested in how they live as Christians in a Muslim country, and he told us the story of his family.

Communicating with him and listening to his story was very interesting, and many topics came up during the discussion.

As I spent this time with Firaz, it never entered my mind that he would later become my husband. When saying goodbye that evening, he asked me for my phone number and suggested that everyone go to the cinema together. Of course, I didn't give my number, nor did I agree to go to the cinema.

A friend later persuaded me to go to the cinema, and another meeting with Firaz took place. This time we exchanged phone numbers, and from that moment we became good friends. We got along great, and we had a great time together. I did not get hung up on who was Christian or who was Catholic or who was from another religion. We felt very good together.

By the way, I had not been thinking about what the fortune-teller predicted about the future love of my life. I did not compare events, and I did not seek out anyone who could fill in that role and become the great love that she had predicted.

Time carried on. We called each other and chatted on the phone.

At first, I was very surprised by his questions. He called me in the mornings and asked if I had breakfast, or to remind me to wear warm clothes because it's cold outside.

I was not accustomed to such dialogue. I was very surprised and thought, *what is your business? Why are you asking about this?* My first husband never asked me about anything like this. We didn't communicate in this way, so it was foreign to me.

He called me several times a day and wondered if I was tired, and advised me to rest. This all seemed like an exaggerated concern. I thought, *what do you want from me?*

At the time, Firaz lived with his older sister. They rented an apartment. Our friendship gradually grew stronger. I succumbed to his charm more and more. I was a little unsettled when he said, "I won't lie to you." I did not immediately understand the meaning of this statement, or what he meant by it.

Visions of divorce from my husband began to visit me. I still talked to him occasionally on the phone, but most of the communication was with my mother. Our telephone calls were not always pleasant, and I began to think about whether it was time to put an end to this relationship.

Apparently, this friendship with Firaz turned something upside down in my head, or some kind of chemical reaction of love began to take place. I didn't think that I had any future here with Firaz, but thanks to him, it was easier for me to end the relationship with my husband back home.

Firaz and I spent time together over the course of two or three months. Once while I was visiting him, I unexpectedly pronounced, "I love you." He looked at me, smiled, hugged me and replied, "I'm sorry. I really like you, but I can't answer you in the same way."

Oh my God! What have I done? I felt like a complete idiot. He continued, "I don't want to lie to you. I really like you, and you're too good of a person to lie to."

Despite this awkward moment, our friendship continued. Later, he and his sister prepared to go on vacation to Syria to meet with their parents and relatives. Before leaving, he bought a big toy bear, came to me, handed it to me and said, "I love you."

Here you go! What is it? One moment you don't love me, the next moment you do? I immediately answered, "Do not lie to me!"

He replied, "You see, love is a feeling, and when it has come you cannot change it. And I don't want to change anything. I love you."

On that day, I spoke with my mother. I asked where my husband was, and she answered, upset, that he was off drinking somewhere. She was very worried. I called my husband and we had a fight on the phone.

I went to the balcony. It was late evening, and the sky was starry and beautiful. I could not stand it and burst into tears. I thought, *how did I get such a life?* Most of all, I do not approve of folly. I would rather listen to this Arab who speaks beautiful words to me, even if I perceive them with some distrust, than to listen to my spouse swear at me on the phone.

I didn't care if I would be alone with my son, or if I found someone else. At that moment, I felt sorry for myself and the decision was made completely.

I immediately called my mom and gave her the news.

I returned to Lithuania. I have more than once considered everything and compared my values to my husband's. At first, I was afraid of him. Then I felt sorry for him, and thought that he would disappear without me. Nevertheless, I revised my priorities. Why should I feel sorry for someone else? Why can't I feel sorry for myself? After all, what will happen to our son growing up in a family with endless conflicts? This situation brought great pain to our son. He did not understand why his mother was not with him. Mom had left to earn money so that he could have a computer or other various things. Both my child and I endured psychological injuries, so I decided to close this page of my life.

I divorced my first husband in 2005. I turned to a lawyer because I could not participate in the court, and everything proceeded in a civilized manner.

I returned to Denmark and continued to work. Sometime in November, my lawyer called and said, "Congratulations, you are now a free woman. You know, I've seen a lot of divorced couples, but I want to tell you that it was not your loss, but his."

I rearranged my life with my loved ones. Firaz proposed to me. By that time, we were already living together, our daughter had been born, and we wanted to legitimize our relationship. My family did not accept this. One of my brothers said he would kill Firaz. We had to endure a lot from both of our families.

It was very important for Firaz that our marriage took place in a church. This is an important part of his culture and customs, and I was not going to challenge his wishes. But the fact was, I had already experienced the wedding ceremony with my first husband.

Therefore, in order to get married in a Catholic church, I had to first get the church to recognize my divorce. It cost a lot of money, nerves, and time. Two years passed until, finally, it happened. As you can see, love prevailed. But along the road to happiness, we went to hell and back.

18. 2005

Firaz's Story

*I*t was the year 2005. I lived my new life and was happy in my own way. I met with friends and continued working. Nothing serious happened, until one particular event.

A friend invited me to visit him. He met a girl from Lithuania and said that she would bring her friend to join us.

I already knew my friend's girlfriend, and we were also friends. When I first arrived and saw her friend Asta, I thought, *Who is this? Who do they want to introduce me to?*

Asta was tall, of dense build, and her hair was strictly combed back. Next to me, she seemed like a giantess, and I didn't like her at all.

I went to my friend and asked him in Arabic, *"Who do you want to introduce me to, this giantess?"*

My friend reassured me that everything was ok, and that it was only for today. "You just stay with us and you don't need anything else!"

I agreed and decided to stay, and we all started talking. I knew a few Russian words, "thank you," and something else. I began to say these words, and Asta asked me why I was speaking Russian, since she is not Russian. As time went by, the conversation didn't improve! The conversation was not flowing. Suddenly, I noticed the funeral of Pope John Paul II was showing on TV, and I became distracted. Asta and her friend were surprised at my interest in the funeral, and asked, "Why are you interested in this? This is a minister of the Christian church."

I responded that I am also a Christian. After that, Asta began talking to me in a different way, and we soon found many things in common. At the end of the evening, I asked Asta if we could meet again. I can't explain, but some kind of chemical reaction had occurred in me. I really wanted to see her again! My prejudices about the *giantess*, the tall woman who was not nice to me, seemed to have evaporated.

Suddenly, everything changed. I wanted to see her! We had so many topics to talk about! We spoke without stopping, each of us telling our own story. We found a lot in common. It was impossible to see at first glance.

19. TURNS OF DESTINY

Firaz's Story

Soon enough Asta and I had met each other several times. I could not stop. I wanted to see her again and again, and I constantly called her on the phone.

We talked about life, we laughed, and we cried together. We were indescribably matched.

Eventually, Asta said that she loved me. I had goosebumps, but I was not sure of my feelings for her at the time. I told her that I would never lie to her. I was afraid to say that I also loved her. She probably didn't like that.

We did love each other, but both Asta and I understood that marriage was impossible because our families would not approve of this relationship. We did not see a shared future.

Our culture is very different from the culture in Lithuania. Moreover, to connect your life with a divorced woman who has a child? No! It was unthinkable.

I was not married, and I had no children. My parents were waiting for me to finally meet an Arab girl and start a family.

I did not want to let them down, and I did not want to offend Asta by giving her false hope for the future. We could not have a future. Culture and customs are very important to me; if I refused them, my family would refuse me.

This is the main reason why I did not confess to Asta's love.

20. PARTING

Firaz's Story

*H*aving evaluated all the obstacles, we decided one day to part ways. But after a month and a half passed, we rushed back to each other in a craze.

My sister and I needed to go to Syria to meet with our family. Having to say goodbye once again loomed ahead. I realized I did not want to lose Asta. That feeling was boiling within me, and I couldn't bear the thought of losing her.

I bought her a toy bear and went to confess my love.

This recognition was very important to me. I never lie, nor do I use my words casually, especially when it comes to something serious.

I was led by my feelings, and I confessed to her my love with enthusiasm and joy. I was ready to fly with her to heaven, soaring over the ocean! I was immensely happy. As a result, Asta moved in to live with me.

We were happy. However, my sister, who I had been living with for years, was not. The situation was resolved because

Asta was very brave and patient. I understand how much patience was necessary to be with me, to live with me, while I was trying to smooth out disagreements with my family. Asta was able to accept the customs and the culture of our people, which was probably not easy. She took everything calmly. Sometimes I was frustrated trying to live up to the standard of my father. Sometimes Asta also broke. She proved to me that I should live life for myself, and not to live trying to satisfy the expectations of my father. Sometimes I think, *why are we still together?* We are probably only together thanks to her patience, and because of the love we share.

I scold myself for a lot of mistakes when remembering the beginning of our relationship. For example, according to tradition, my sister's needs must come first. If Asta and I sat together in a park and my sister called wanting me to come, I would apologize and leave Asta to be with my sister.

For a while, I always rushed back and forth between my beloved woman and my sister.

I explained to my sister that I want to live with Asta, but she did not agree. She insisted that I should find an Arab girl, not a stranger!

My family was also angry with me for being with a foreigner. My father did not recognize our relationship. He asked, "Who is Asta for you?"

Being afraid of my father, I told him that Asta is only a friend, a girl with whom I spend time. He reminded me, "Do you remember who you are? You have no future with this woman! You can only spend time with her, nothing more."

One day, I finally decided to take a bold step. I left my sister, rented another apartment and took Asta to live with me.

My niece told everything to my father. Only with time did he become more understanding. He probably understood me in his heart, but the rest of the family still did not recognize my decision. They have not talked to me for a year. Only my mother, and occasionally my sister, violated this unwritten rule.

While Asta and I proved to everyone that we have the right to our love, a lot of time passed.

21. SOLUTION FOR THE LOVE DILEMMA

Firaz's Story

*A*sta and I lived together for two years. When she became pregnant, I decided to go to Lithuania to meet her relatives and ask for her hand in marriage. This is customary in our culture. Although I was aware of the hostile attitude her family held towards me, in the end, we went to Lithuania together. When her relatives gathered, her brother laughed and asked, "What do you want?"

I explained that I love Asta and I want to live with her for the rest of my life.

Asta's mom accepted me as a son. I really love my mother-in-law; she is like a mother to me.

On August 31, 2008, our daughter was born. We were happy. One day, my family called me from Jordan and informed me that my father had been diagnosed with cancer and was seriously ill. I was asked to come urgently. I began to say that I couldn't come right away because I would have to take leave from work. But my brother told me that it's all the same with my work, that my father was dying, and that

I must buy a ticket and come! So, I went to say goodbye to my father. He died in a hospital. After that, my mother and my sister's family went to live in America.

After the funeral, I returned to Denmark. It was a difficult time for my soul, and I spent a lot of time in thought. I thought about Asta, about our new daughter, and about myself, and I realized that this is exactly the woman with whom I want to live, until death do us part. Asta and our daughter are my real family!

I have been waiting for my beloved for seven years! She gave me a daughter, and now I can't live without my family.

My cousins remained angry and tried to reason with me. I said to them, "You do not pay for my apartment. You do not buy me food. You do not pay my expenses. Why should I listen to you?"

I offered Asta my hand and my heart, and we registered our marriage in Copenhagen in 2010. I made the difficult decision to introduce her to my family. I felt that Asta would be loved. She is a very nice and friendly person. She always treats everyone with love, and always comes to the aid of those in need.

Therefore, after Lithuania, our whole family went to Jordan to see my relatives. And, as I expected, all my relatives immediately fell in love with Asta. She became an equal member of the family.

In 2012, we decided to seal our marriage in a church. It was an important moment for me, and for my family. I was happy that Asta agreed to this step. This meant that we would testify our union to higher powers.

Asta and I went through a lot of trouble until we received consent from the church for our wedding. In the end, our wedding was amazing. These are unforgettable moments.

22. FIRAZ

Asta's Story

Religion can play a big role in any family. By connecting your life with a person of a different faith, you must adapt in many ways. My new love was a man of a different nationality, and I had to accept it.

We do not go to church too often, neither he nor I. However, we do celebrate Christmas and Easter.

Since he is Orthodox and I am Catholic, our religious holidays differ only in dates. Moreover, my husband notes all holidays according to Catholic and Orthodox customs. He grew up in a family where all religious traditions were very strictly observed.

I always say that I do not know what will happen tomorrow; I live very well in the here and now. After all, no one knows their future. What will it be? And what is worth hoping for? It may not be exactly what you expect.

I lived with my Lithuanian husband for fifteen years. The same culture, the same religion. I have been living with a person of a different nationality for nearly sixteen years. And I am happy! It's quite a paradox.

I believe that there is one very important thing in the relationship between a man and a woman. If people want to be together, they must accept both culture and religion. They will agree on some things, disagree on others, and close their eyes altogether in some areas. Sometimes they will remain silent, and it will be taken for granted. It would be a desire!

I can't say that it's easy. But over time, all the sharp corners are gently smoothed out and don't seem so sharp. They will be "polished" by mutual effort. And this is the most valuable thing in the family.

Now I live happily ever after. But to get to this point, I had to endure very difficult circumstances. At first, we had a lot of disagreements. There were turning points for me and for him. Religion was not the sole cause of trouble, but it was another aspect.

We Europeans, as a rule, have a negative attitude towards men from Middle Eastern countries. We only know about the very bad experiences of other women with men of these nationalities.

I used to have a very bad opinion of Arabs. I even wrote about this to my friend. She had been dating a friend of the man who would become my husband. He is the one who introduced us.

My friend probably still has that letter. I wrote: "Do you understand what you are doing? Run away from him as far as possible! He will ruin your life! He is Arab!"

I always had a negative opinion about mixed marriages. And even now, such thoughts can occasionally slip through. This is because there are many couples who cannot get along. Their religion and culture prevail, and families become destroyed. These couples cannot find a compromise. And all because they do not speak the language of love. They do not want to talk, and they are driven only by ambition.

23. EXPERIENCE

Asta's Story

I lived for fifteen years with a Lithuanian man, and now I have been living with an Arab man for thirteen years. I can say that the differences are as distinct as those between heaven and earth.

I am not saying that we have no quarrels or problems. Of course, we do. But we do not fight or throw dishes. We always stop in time, and we never cross the line.

This does not mean that all Arab people are good, or that all Lithuanians are bad. In any nation there are both good and bad people. And in general, the matter is not one of nationality, but of the person themselves. Everything matters! What was his upbringing? What type of family did he grow up in? Here, even seemingly simple household trifles matter.

There are different life stories.

In the beginning, when we had just met, I specifically told my friends, "He is an Arab!" I liked to watch their response.

I even provoked those who asked me with whom I live. My loved ones did not approve, but that didn't bother me much.

They did not know what I knew! And this reality gave me wings. No fakes, masks, or powders. I was ready to scream with joy, "I'm in love! I love you!"

Time passed, but our love only grew stronger. His kisses have driven me crazy for many years. Who hasn't dreamed of this? Now the dream is my life. My reality!

AFTERWORD

*T*hrough wisdom, I managed to endure.

I only know one thing:

Life is beautiful, and we create it in accordance with our capabilities.

Thank you for our family. I am thankful that my loved ones and I are healthy.

I'm happy.

I am blessed as a wife.

I cannot want more, because I have everything that I need to be happy.

Firaz, my love, every day I love you more and more!

Your love and care support me every second.

For more information
about the author, please visit:

www.storiesaldona.eu/en/

Facebook: aldona.grupas
Instagram: aldonagrupas
Or email: aldonagr@gmail.com

ABOUT THE AUTHOR

*A*ldona Grupas was born in Riga, Latvia, to Lithuanian parents.

In 1976, she moved with her family to Klaipeda, the third largest city in Lithuania, where she lived for most of her life before moving to the United Kingdom in 2005.

She studied nursing in college in Klaipeda and began her nursing career in 1979. She also studied law at Riga University of Law from 2001 to 2005.

She moved to the UK in 2005 and has worked in a nursing home since, where she has met many people and authored books on the topic.

With every donation, a voice will be given to the creativity that lies within the hearts of our children living with diverse challenges.

By making this difference, children that may not have been given the opportunity to have their Heart Heard will have the freedom to create beautiful works of art and musical creations.

Donate by visiting

HeartstobeHeard.com

We thank you.